FERN HILL

FOR MIXED CHORUS, MEZZO-SOPRANO SOLO AND ORCHESTRA

MUSIC BY
JOHN CORIGLIANO

POEM BY
DYLAN THOMAS

Vocal Score

G. SCHIRMER, INC./NEW YORK

ED. 2485

Fern Hill *was first performed on December 19, 1961 at Carnegie Recital Hall by the chorus and orchestra of the Manhattan School of Music under the direction of Hugh Ross.*

THE FOLLOWING INSTRUMENTIONS ARE AVAILABLE
ON RENTAL FROM THE PUBLISHER:

1. Strings, piano and harp (optional)

2. Full orchestra

APPROXIMATE TIME: 16 MINUTES

FERN HILL

Now as I was young and easy under the apple boughs
About the lilting house and happy as the grass was green,
   The night above the dingle starry,
     Time let me hail and climb
   Golden in the heydays of his eyes,
And honoured among wagons I was prince of the apple towns
And once below a time I lordly had the trees and leaves
     Trail with daisies and barley
   Down the rivers of the windfall light.

And as I was green and carefree, famous among the barns
About the happy yard and singing as the farm was home,
   In the sun that is young once only,
     Time let me play and be
   Golden in the mercy of his means,
And green and golden I was huntsman and herdsman, the calves
Sang to my horn, the foxes on the hills barked clear and cold,
     And the sabbath rang slowly
   In the pebbles of the holy streams.

All the sun long it was running, it was lovely, the hay
Fields high as the house, the tunes from the chimneys, it was air
   And playing, lovely and watery
     And fire green as grass.
   And nightly under the simple stars
As I rode to sleep the owls were bearing the farm away,
All the moon long I heard, blessed among stables, the nightjars
     Flying with the ricks, and the horses
     Flashing into the dark.

And then to awake, and the farm, like a wanderer white
With the dew, come back, the cock on his shoulder: it was all
   Shining, it was Adam and maiden,
     The sky gathered again
   And the sun grew round that very day.
So it must have been after the birth of the simple light
In the first, spinning place, the spellbound horses walking warm
     Out of the whinnying green stable
     On to the fields of praise.

And honoured among foxes and pheasants by the gay house
Under the new made clouds and happy as the heart was long,
   In the sun born over and over
     I ran my heedless ways,
   My wishes raced through the house high hay
And nothing I cared, at my sky blue trades, that time allows
In all his tuneful turning so few and such morning songs
     Before the children green and golden
     Follow him out of grace.

Nothing I cared, in the lamb white days, that time would take me
Up to the swallow thronged loft by the shadow of my hand,
   In the moon that is always rising,
     Nor that riding to sleep
   I should hear him fly with the high fields
And wake to the farm forever fled from the childless land.
Oh as I was young and easy in the mercy of his means,
     Time held me green and dying
   Though I sang in my chains like the sea.

For B. Tillis

Fern Hill

(For Mixed Chorus, Mezzo-Soprano Solo and Orchestra)

Dylan Thomas*

John Corigliano

Fern Hill, Copyright 1945, by Dylan Thomas. Used by permission of Harold Ober Associates, Inc.

45267C

4

Now   as   I   was   young   and

SOPRANO

ALTO

TENOR

BASS

*optional cut from 𝄴 to 𝄵

6

45267

*Alto II more marcato than Alto I

16

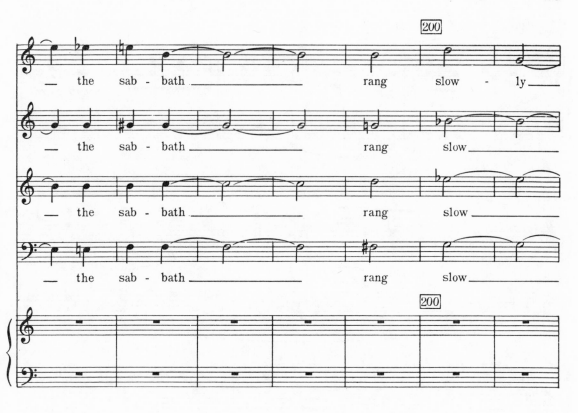

long I heard, blessed a-mong sta-bles, the night-jars Fly-ing with the ricks, and the hors-es Flash-ing in-to the dark.

The sky gath - ered a - gain And the sun grew round that ver - y day.

310

SOPRANO

aft - er the birth of the sim - ple light

ALTO

So it must have been aft - er the birth of the sim - ple light

TENOR

So it must have been aft - er the birth of the sim - ple light

BASS

In the

* or small choir

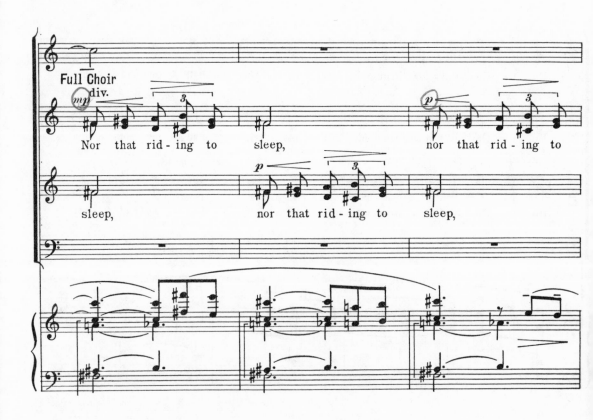